Be Unstoppable in Life, Relationships and Business with Self-Hypnosis the Easy Way

All about Self-Hypnosis and how it can help you become Wealthy, Healthy, and Powerful

David Anton

Be Unstoppable in Life, Relationships and Business with Self-Hypnosis the Easy Way

ISBN 978-1517760977

Table of Contents

How a young 16 year old found the power of hypnosis by reading a 77 year old masterpiece

I'm sure you have read Napoleon Hill's masterpiece, Think and Grow Rich.

In the book, Hill goes to a lot of trouble explaining auto-suggestion, or self-hypnosis. That's where I first got the hypnosis bug.

While I was only 16 at the time, (lucky for me an early mentor gave me a copy of Think and Grow Rich to read), I was hooked for life to seek self and INNER improvement.

After thoroughly digesting the limited resources of my high-school library on hypnosis I started to find other esoteric trails that led me to fasting, meditation and eventually to how to 'cycle' myself into the 'outer world' through various methods.

But it all started through Hypnosis. And that's the subject of this book.

I want to get right to the meat of the book quickly, so I'm not going to spend a lot of time on the background or history of our subject matter, since most of that is not really important, and is, in my opinion just a lot of fluff that you can get from reading a Wikipedia post.

IMPORTANT NOTE: I'll be showing you how you can really take a giant leap forward in hypnosis, in the last chapter, although I'll be hinting at it throughout. You can save a lot of time and money with this amazing short cut, and or, create specialized hypnosis sessions for yourself, or as a business.

So let's delve in and discover…

What Hypnosis is and What Can It Do for You

Here is a somewhat boring definition for something so very powerful:

"A cooperative interaction where the participant responds to the suggestions of the hypnotist."

While the definition of hypnosis may vary from practitioner to practitioner, this definition of the American Psychological Association will suit us.

True, hypnosis has been very popular 'thanks' to well-known stage-acts – where a hypnotist with the showmanship skills of P.T. Barnum finds willing audience members to perform unusual or even ridiculous actions (running around the stage barking like a dog, acting as if they lost their wallet, or that their pants are on fire – I remember laughing a bit watching a stage hypnotist performing this in an open air performance – I was very young at the time and was not as mature as I am today, but even back then I wondered, 'if I could make people believe their pants were on fire, could I make them believe their health was better, or that they could play football better?), there's a lot more benefits to be gained from hypnosis than just earning a living as an entertainer.

While I admit it was fun as a teenager to practice what I had learned, for my immature amusement, (nothing malicious), I quickly grew out of that stage and began to look beyond the childish entertainment aspects of the art, and how I could help myself and others with this (seemingly to me) amazing power.

In fact, since leaving my teens, I have never personally participated in anything even remotely 'entertaining'.

Everything I have worked on, produced, or people I have hypnotized has been for their good, and my own financial good as well.

Remember, there is nothing wrong with being paid for helping others achieve their goals.

Besides using hypnosis for esoteric purposes, it has been repeatedly and clinically proven to provide medical and therapeutic benefits. Most notably, it has been used in significantly reducing pain, anxiety, as well as toning down the symptoms of dementia.

Further, many athletic trainers use hypnosis to assist their athletes getting into peek perfection.

Spy agencies use hypnosis also, to train operatives to resist questioning and lie-detector technologies. Today, many corporations are facing industrial espionage, and I can see businesses using hypnosis to ferret out spies and to protect their own spies as well.

Students use it to prepare for exams, and business people use it to get an edge in their professions.

One can even use hypnosis to help in your love life or sex life.

There is really nothing that you cannot use hypnosis to benefit you in.

The Process of Hypnosis Explained

When you hear the term 'hypnotist', what is the first thing that comes to your mind? For many and, perhaps, for you too, such a word may bring up images of a sinister-looking villain, performing on the stage, swinging a clock or pendulum back and forth, and ultimately, making other people do his dark bidding.

One wonders if Anton Mesmer, one of the first serious practitioners of the modern era appeared dressed like our image of a hypnotist for theatrical reasons, or just because that's how most men dressed in that period.

If you were to dress like Mesmer today, you would look a bit theatrical.

Marvelous feats in Mind Reading.

If Mesmer were alive today, he would probably just let Hugo Boss take care of his appearance, (no doubt a wealthy woman would be picking up that tab, knowing him!).

However, real hypnosis bears very little resemblance to these Hollywood portrayals and stereotyped images or Mesmer imitators.

Kreskin was a master hypnotist, on television for years, and yet looked more like a Colombo than a Mesmer.

According to Kihlstrom, the hypnotist does not really put the subject or person under hypnosis. Instead, the hypnotist acts more like a coach...a tutor. His primary job is to help the person become hypnotized.

However, I still think something is missing from our definition.

In my opinion being under a hypnosis-state or trance state is very close to sleep. In fact, those who have been hypnotized report a great relaxation after being brought out of their state, very akin to a great sleep – another 'blessing' of that art.

A much better characterization of hypnosis is that it's a state that results in sharper and focused attention, vivid fantasies, as well as increased suggestibility.

And that is the key, because it's all about getting past the 'gate-keeper.'

The 'gate-keeker' you ask?

Our conscious mind, our rational mind that tells us we 'can't do that' – that stops most of us from living in the Now, from fulfilling our dreams, from achieving our goals, or even finding that love of our life.

Remember the last time you drove home from the office and you got out of your car, and could not even remember details of the drive home?

That is because your subconscious mind was able to perform most of the actions for you. Perhaps you were deep in thought, or talking on the phone, but you were trusting your subconscious mind to take you safely home, and it did.

Simple, yet POWERFUL – some people can't drive a car with ALL their attention – yet you could not even remember the trip home! That means you can let your subconscious take over once you've programmed it.

This is the Zen edge that the Masters of any profession have – or spiritual leaders have achieved, sometimes they don't even know it, sometimes they think it's some secret system or talent that only they have, but it's not.

It's just that they now perform in the Success Zone, that mental state of consciousness where the subconscious has taken charge.

If you want a jump start to success, you can get it with hypnosis.

You see, it's not just about solving problems, i.e. getting over a phobia, dealing with health issues, it's about taking someone who is at a 'good' level in their chosen field, and making them GREAT!

For me, that was the power that I was able to unleash – and you can have it too.

But I'm getting ahead of myself.

Hypnosis – What's In It For You?

What you experience during hypnosis differs, sometimes dramatically, from others.

Some individuals who were hypnotized reported feeling a sense of detachment from what's happening around them.

Others experienced extreme relaxation.

Plus, there are cases where subjects feel that their actions while under hypnosis was outside of their consciousness.

On the contrary, there are individuals that are fully aware...even able to carry out conversations while under the power of hypnosis.

The bottom line is this: each of our experiences under hypnosis can vary... but if we are guided right, can be rich and very beneficial.

However, each of these feelings is not too dissimilar, and once you have used hypnosis often, you can find that each of the sessions makes you relaxed, yet, when finished, ready to go to the next step (i.e. you could now just fall asleep, or if you do your routine in the morning, jump out of bed feeling like you can take on the world – and you'll have the mindset now to do it!

Throughout the years, hypnosis has been elevated from something mystical and unknown to a very useful tool in the field of psychology and medicine.

Here are just some of the few applications of hypnosis that have been uncovered and thoroughly demonstrated through research:

- Treating chronic and painful conditions like rheumatoid arthritis.

- Attuning the ability to better practice esoteric arts

- Being able to talk to members of the opposite sex and succeed

•   Surgery-free treatment and significant reduction of pain during and after child-birth.

•   Improving your Golf, Tennis, Hockey, Body-building etc. performance

•   Significant reduction of the effects and symptoms of dementia.

•   Deepening the Law of Attraction within you

•   As for ADHD, a condition that can plague children and adults alike, hypnosis can be very helpful in toning down its effects.

•   Changing your attitude about money

•   Patients who underwent chemotherapy and are suffering from nausea and vomiting can be significantly helped through consistent hypnotherapy.

•   Changing your attitude about sex

•   Reduction and even total elimination of skin conditions that almost everyone is suffering from like warts, psoriasis, and more.

•   Being a better student, sales person, realtor, day trader, and other professions

•   IBS symptoms and effects can be toned down to a very low level through hypnosis.

Now, don't get it wrong. Hypnosis is not the Holy Grail that will cure every problem of mankind.   But there is not a problem facing man that hypnosis can't help in one way or another.

However, if you haven't considered hypnosis as an option for improving your life in general, then you are missing out.

In fact, let me say, it is much easier to improve a specific weakness in your life, or, conversely, to enhance something you already do well, so you can reach perfection.

If you'd like a free Law of Attraction Hypnosis sample, just visit www.professionalastrologycenter.info – note it's .info, NOT dot 'com.'

4 HUGE Questions about Hypnosis and Hypnotherapy that you can't escape

While accepted as a valid medical procedure by the American Medical Association in 1958, I have discovered that hypnosis/hypnotherapy remains shrouded in mystery.

I remember chatting to a girl I had just met in a coffee shop. I thought we were getting along, and wanted to ask her out. She asked me what I did for a living, and I said I was a type of therapist, a hypo –therapist.

Bang. It was as if I let out the longest, loudest, wettest fart.

She looked at me like I was some sort of weirdo. It seems that the image of that old man with a goatee and coat, swinging a pendulum back and forth to render his victims helpless, is really hard to shake off. Maybe I should have dressed like that and told her I was a rock star, or poet.

Needless to say I never had coffee with her again.

But I did make a mental note to be more circumspect when explaining to people what I did for a living.

And the stage performances of hypnotists – making other people walk as if they were standing on burning coal, run around the hall like nuts, etc., certainly didn't help our unfairly dubious reputation.

NOTE: having said that, I've taught the whole hot coal walking exercise however it has nothing to do with hypnosis.

BUT when people set aside those inflexible notions about hypnosis, and focus on what it can really do for their well-being the results are amazing.

Let's cover some of the biggest and most common questions about hypnosis just so you have the answers ready to deliver:

Really, What Is Hypnosis?

Contrary to popular belief, hypnosis is not sleep. However, it's a natural, really relaxed, and focused state of mind. It is usually characterized by feelings of well-being, increased muscle relaxation, predominating alpha brain waves, and more.

Okay, okay, while that sounds like a dictionary, read it again, because it's very powerful. Because once you are into that state, you have past the gate-keeper.

What it does is it puts you in a state where one gains the ability to accept new ideas and beliefs (and break older and negative ones) if they are sufficiently emotionalized and doesn't go against your inner values.

Now remember, while your subconscious is receiving these messages, one session is usually not even remotely enough to create a change.

Many people give up before their subconscious had a chance of changing or re-arraigning the neurons in their brains to get to where they want. While hypnosis itself is a major short cut to success, there is no short-cut to the practice.

People spend years in bad behavior but want 'McDonald's speed' in getting 'better'.

The harder a bad behavior is engrained in us, the more sessions you need. Don't let someone say to you, 'Well, I tried a couple of sessions, (or 7), and still I'm smoking.'

Smoking is so physically addictive, that it does take a serious amount of hypnosis sessions to affect change. That's just one example.

But the good news is that hypnosis is not a drug, there are no 'side effects', and by using the technology available with recorded sessions, you can save a ton of money for yourself, or for your clients.

Bottom line is hypnosis is one of the most powerful short-cuts to success, achievement, or as a curative, possible.

In a nutshell, hypnosis is either of the two things: (1) an interactive and guided imagery, or (2) highly focused and applied meditations while in various levels of trance, all geared towards a specific and worthwhile goal – and you can achieve so much – there is just no limit to what you can do!

Let's look at some common examples:

Will It Help Me Drop Smoking and Lose Weight or 'fill in the blank'?

While there is solid and measured proof showing that hypnotherapy can be a very effective tool in getting rid of your nicotine addiction and/or losing those unwanted pounds, there is one very important factor comes into play: your desire to change.

Hypnosis can't make you do something that, deep down, you don't really want to do! You cannot hypnotize someone out of the blue to run a marathon…unless they were already a runner.

Put it this way: hypnosis is like a hammer. On its own, it cannot drive a nail through a piece of wood. But with you and your desire moving that hammer, it's a whole lot easier than just using your hands.

However: Hypnosis can increase your will-power in creating the DESIRE for change… i.e. lose weight.

So, if you feel you, or someone you are coaching, or working with does not have the 100% desire to achieve the goal their conscious mind wishes to increase that you can use hypnosis to create a real desire on your part for change.

Good examples are smoking and losing weight, but also focus on work, on practicing an activity, like learning to play the piano, working out, studying math (yes, I used that one myself!), etc.

Don't get stuck into this 'well, if I don't want to be helped I can't be helped' mode, because if you know you want to change hypnosis is going to work for you – even if you think you can't resist that last piece of pie!

Will Hypnosis/Hypnotherapy Put People In Danger?

The answer is a big NO.

Matter of fact, the Council of Mental Health of the American Medical Association gave hypnosis its seal of approval as a safe practice…a valid medical tool that has no harmful side effects back in September 1958. To date, there are no reports of a subject getting seriously hurt with hypnosis.

Look, cars hurt more people than planes, yet more people are afraid to fly than to drive. Alcohol kills more Americans than guns. Yet some people are afraid of hypnosis.

The way I look at it, is a bit weird.

The fact that this amazingly powerful agent of help is feared or scoffed at by most people makes it a big plus for those of us who use it.

If you want to get ahead in your profession, and most of your professional colleagues are afraid to use hypnosis or don't even realize it's something they can use to earn more, or succeed with, you are going to be far ahead of the pack.

You don't have to tell anyone your secret for getting to the top quickly.

And if you are a practitioner, you can really help your clients move forward. What a big plus you can offer!

It All Sounds Nice, BUT Can I Be Hypnotized?

Studies reveal that almost everyone can be hypnotized. There are only 3 types of people that cannot be (and in some cases, shouldn't be) hypnotized:

- Someone suffering from a thought disorder or psychotic process (whose thinking of their 'ex' right now?)

- Someone with a low IQ

- Someone who just doesn't want to be hypnotized (you know, that annoying friend or brother-in-law who always has something snarky to say)

If you want to be hypnotized, if you are willing to participate in the process, and if you can use your imagination or improvise, you can be hypnotized.

And of course, if you are not smart enough, well, you have other problems.

To date I've never working with anyone who I had to turn away.

Getting the idea here?

Using hypnosis is like having your own secret weapon for your success!

Hey, if you'd like a free Law of Attraction Hypnosis sample, just visit www.professionalastrologycenter.info – note it's .info, NOT dot 'com.'

3 Most Important Uses of Self-Hypnosis you should know about before getting into the game

You have an hour or so where you can do anything you want. What would you do? Does watching TV sound good? Maybe you prefer to spend that hour surfing the net, or 'working' on Facebook?

Well, here's an even better suggestion: use self-hypnosis and make your life a notch or two better each time! You see, self-hypnosis is a very natural process that we experience...it's as natural as breathing and sleeping.

Matter of fact, every one of us enters this trance state that results to heightened awareness and suggestibility coupled with extreme relaxation day in and day out! Whenever you first wake up in the morning and just before you go to bed, you are in this trance state.

This is the time Napoleon Hill wrote about in his books, (both Think and Grow Rich and his 17 volume work Laws of Success). Men like Andrew Carnegie, Henry Ford and JD Rockefeller knew and used auto-suggestion (as they called it or self-hypnosis – surely they knew something about success!)

Whenever you are doing something that's really absorbing you like reading a very interesting book, you are in a hypnotic trance. But here's the thing, only a handful can use this trance state to positively change their lives. Don't you want to be one of these open-minded people?

Here are some of the 3 things that self-hypnosis can do for you to change your life for the better:

Get Rid Of Negative Beliefs

I used to be an arrogant, self-important know it all, so I went to a hypnotist to see if he could help me.

Now I'm perfect.

How we react to events all depend on our beliefs and the emotions we subconsciously link to it. If you have a terrible first-time public speaking experience, it's very likely that your fear of speaking to strangers or shaking hands came from it.

Fear of public speaking is one of the main areas from which I get business clients.

If you are going to succeed in business you MUST learn to speak to groups. From boardrooms to ballrooms, if you want to lead in business you must lead from the front of the room.

What about general self-confidence?

Are you someone who believes that you are not good enough?

Perhaps you think that all men are cheats?

Or all women are out to get your money?

Such negative beliefs can seriously damage your quality of life. In fact, it will destroy any chance you have for a quality life.

With self-hypnosis, such negative emotions, beliefs, and associations can be easily eliminated PERMANENTLY.

While those are just a few examples, if you plan to be a successful practitioner of any kind of esoteric art, you must be the example to your clients.

There is nothing worse for a client than to lose belief in his practitioner because they feel 'sorry' for them.

Your client will have no confidence in you if they feel you are in a worse situation then they are – especially if you are offering help.

The term 'physician heal thyself' applies to esoteric practitioners as well.

Bottom line: self-hypnosis, (and I include the use of recorded hypnotic sessions that specifically target areas of concern here as part of self-hypnosis) can eliminate negative beliefs and offer people an even chance.

Now, if you want an 'unfair advantage', read on to the next section, 'cause this you gonna love!

Installing New and Positive Beliefs!

Just as important as weeding out the negative beliefs is planting new and positive ones.

Think about it: what if you have the belief system of someone success-ful…say like Bill Gates? How do you think you would feel and act to-wards work? Would it make you more productive and confident in your ability to face challenges and perform tasks at hand? Would it help you make more money and have fun in the process?

Hell yeah it would! And with self-hypnosis, you can easily implant such beliefs in your subconscious thanks to the heightened awareness and suggestibility that the hypnosis-induced trance brings.

Think of any person, alive or from history, that you wish you could emulate. If you know their system for success, power, achievement or creativity, you can have it.

I once had a client who desired to emulate his personal hero, Napoleon. Not Napoleon Hill, as I first thought he meant, but THE Napoleon, Napoleon Bonaparte.

Wow, did this guy want to become the next Emperor of France?

I was wondering, because he lived in Ohio.

So rather than dismiss him, (because I would not help anyone become anything that I felt was morally wrong), I asked him what he thought about when he thought about Napoleon.

I shut my mouth and listened.

What I learned floored me!

It turns out that Napoleon was sort of the 'Tony Robbins' of his day, there are a few quotes of his that I used in my research, to create a very special hypnosis program for this discerning client.

- A leader is a dealer in hope.
- Take time to deliberate, but when the time for action has arrived, stop thinking and go in.
- He who fears being conquered is sure of defeat.
- Victory belongs to the most persevering.
- The truest wisdom is a resolute determination.
- In politics stupidity is not a handicap.
- There are only two forces that unite men - fear and interest.
- Music is the voice that tells us that the human race is greater than it knows.
- Impossible is a word to be found only in the dictionary of fools.
- Great ambition is the passion of a great character. Those endowed with it may perform very good or very bad acts. All depends on the principles which direct them.
- Ten people who speak make more noise than ten thousand who are silent.

If you know what you are doing, there is nothing you cannot create a hypnosis program on.

I love self-hypnosis for this reason, and have helped thousands of people with my specially prepared programs.

Sorry, the Napoleon CD is NOT for sale!

Alleviating Pain and Other Medical Uses

As I've stated before, hypnosis has been recognized as a valid medical tool by the American Medical Association back in September 1958. Since then, more and more medical and psychological uses of self-hypnosis have been uncovered.

In fact, one of my earliest experiences with hypnosis – at a very tender age - was with a friend's father named Hue.

His father was a practicing psychologist who happened to mention he was attending a weekend training on simple hypnosis. My ears perked up, and I asked if I could be his first 'Guinee-pig' when he returned?

Once he was sure that there were no problems with my parents about it, he agreed, and the following week I visited their home again.

Up until then, all I knew about hypnosis was found in books, and/or on TV. I remember making a typical idiotic crack hoping he would not make me run around the house like a chicken with her head cut off.

While I was laughing, he took it seriously, and said 'I hope you know that I would never do such a thing.'

I smartened up and listened to him.

First, I thought he would put me into a trance or sleep like state where I would have tuned out everything else and hear only him. I brought a tape recorder, (one of those 'shoe box' type cassette recorders by Radio Shack)

But no, he told me I'd be awake and aware the entire time.

He when through his steps, and long story short, he had me raise my right arm.

Now I remember, vividly, this episode. I knew I could have lowered my arm anytime, yet, I did not want to, I knew what was happening around me, I could hear noises in the surrounding rooms, I never felt 'carried away' or that I was in a 'trance' yet, he had me raise my arm.

From that day on I was hooked.

I knew then and there that this was a powerful medium for change.

I wanted to be able to use self-hypnosis – that way I did not need to depend on anyone else, so I made a lifelong study into the practice, and consider myself an expert.

Self-hypnosis has helped people with a wide variety of issues; everything from relieving the pain and hot flashes experienced by cancer survivors, performing dental procedures without the use of anesthesia, reducing nausea and vomiting after chemotherapy, hypnosis has shown its power.

Matter of fact, self-hypnosis has been used by soon-to-be non-smokers to get rid of the nicotine addiction that's been plaguing them for decades.

Still self-hypnosis is not an end-all-be-all solution to all of our problems. BUT without a doubt, it has a lot of uses and benefits that everyone, including you, should use on a daily basis!

Maybe it's about time we get rid of the image of a sinister-looking hypnotist we see in Hollywood movies and let the benefits of hypnosis help us make our lives better.

Today you can just use a pre-recorded MP3 and listen to a session to help and advance you.

Powerful stuff!

If you'd like a free Law of Attraction Hypnosis sample, just visit www.professionalastrologycenter.info – note it's .info, NOT dot 'com.'

How to Get In the Best Shape of Your Life with Self-Hypnosis and Guided Imagery

Being a professional athlete can be worth millions to you. Much has been written about Tiger Woods' father's use of hypnosis and subliminals on the young Tiger so I'll not repeat it here. But the fact remains, if you or a client want to get into the best shape to succeed at your chosen athletic practice, than you need to use hypnosis.

It's easy to take sports performance to the next level and even speed up your physical healing process using your mind if you follow the following simple system, or, easier still to use pre-recorded MP3s.

The age-old adage: "Where the mind goes, the body will follow" is very true with self-hypnosis and imagery.

How Is Self-Hypnosis and Imagery different when used for sports?

Self-hypnosis and imagery (sometimes called visualization, mental rehearsal, etc.) refers to specific mental techniques that are used by psychologists and hypnotherapists to help subjects visualize or mentally rehearse an event they want to happen.

This involves using all of the subject's senses to create an imagined experience...one that feels so real. By doing so...by bringing all of your senses in action, you create a very real experience of having your desired outcome or event.

In this case, a complex task of striking a ball, or hitting a puck, or whatever the task of the body to affect a correct outcome, (goal, hole-in-one, 'right-hook' etc) is broken down into each subcomponent.

Tony Robbins and other NLP practitioners use this same method and hypnotic talk to coach athletes.

From there the 'mental rehearsal' or concrete visualization is now your blue-print for success. Once you or your client is in a trance, each step is visualized to the point where the recipient actually feels they are completing each task. Rinse and repeat and you'll be in the Olympics.

Let's break it down some more

How to Use Self-Hypnosis and Imagery – A Simple Step-By-Step Guide

When using self-hypnosis for the first time, it's very helpful to have the process facilitated by a seasoned practitioner. It's always helpful to have someone walk you through the process of guided imagery. You can use CDs, tapes, record your own script if you know the nuts and bolts of the process, etc. After you are comfortable with this mental technique, it's easier to use and practice these mental tools on your own.

(1) Find a comfortable place where you can sit or lay down without any interruptions.

(2) Relax your body. Close your eyes and take several long and slow breaths. Research has revealed that one can quickly change from being restless...panicking to relaxing just by changing his breathing pattern.

(3) After you have deeply relaxed, now is the time to create a vivid and convincing image. This image should be one that you have previously experienced or one that you desire to happen.

Perhaps you want to visualize yourself making that perfect golf swing, landing one hole-in-one after another. Maybe you want to see yourself pumped and all geared up for your basketball game, and ultimately, winning it.

This is where most first timers get a little stumped. But don't worry. Move on to the next step...

(4) Break down the task in to smaller and smaller sub-tasks and visualize each one being expertly managed (you will have to know your sport well enough to know these tasks)

(5) If you are suddenly distracted or thinking about something else, don't worry. Simply acknowledge it and let it go. Focus some more on your breathing pattern if you lose the image, and go back to step 3.

(6) Throughout the session, it's very important to maintain a very positive attitude. Another key point here is that your imagined experience

should be very vivid and complete – with sights, sounds, tastes, feelings, and even how your peak sports performance would smell!

Always take note of the following questions: What are you wearing? Who is in the experience? What do you hear? How do you feel? Now, if your self-hypnosis session isn't going as planned, open your eyes for a while and start all over again with your breathing.

Athletes have A LOT of opportunities to use self-hypnosis and guided imagery to improve their performance. From injury recovery, taking their performance to the next level, gearing up for victory, and more, these mental techniques should be a standard part of an athlete's training program!

A good over all CD or MP3 of your athletic professional is good to use each night and each morning, even if you say 'but I have heard it all before, I can repeat it backwards and forwards.' This matters not, keep listening, especially in those evening and morning hours, as the gate-keeper is not as active and you are getting this information directly into your subconscious. Powerful.

And consider this, what is your opponent listing to? The nightly or morning news? Filling their subconscious with negativity?

Be a professional and feed your brain what it needs to make you number 1.

NOTE: you MUST know the steps for success, i.e. the steps for a perfect tennis serve, or a long drive in golf, etc. If you know them, write them out and be sure you have not missed any before creating your own session.

And FYI, you can google 'Hypnosis scripts' and find a ton of scripts that will guide you into the relaxed state, from there you just need to create your own steps to a successful outcome, and lastly, use a script to bring you back out of your trance-like state.

If you'd like a free Law of Attraction Hypnosis sample, just visit www.professionalastrologycenter.info – note it's .info, NOT dot 'com.'

Sleeping Better and Getting More Out Of Your Bed Time with Hypnotherapy

I think I'm a bit of a hypnotist.

Every time I'm in bed with my wife and I mention sex, she falls into a deep sleep.

Here's the bad news: chronic sleep disorders are plaguing millions of Americans every year... and chances are, you just might be one of them.

Of course, if you plan to become someone that helps those with any of these challenges than this could be considered good news – there is lots of business out there!

In any event, it's a serious problem not only in America, but world-wide.

Now, don't think that the old story about the person with the worse shoes being the cobbler isn't' true.

I remember, just a year ago, I when through a period of sleeplessness. I was so fed up with it that I was about to make an appointment to see the doctor, when I was scanning some of the testimonials I get from people who use my hypnosis MP3s and saw one from Betty.

Betty was a real insomniac. For years she tried all sorts of drugs, which only worked up to a point, she would either take one tablet and fall asleep, only to wake up at 4 AM and stay awake for the rest of the day, but still be dog-tired, or, she would take a pill and find that it just made her tired all day. Nothing worked, until she tried one of my CDs.

So it hit me, I started to listen to my own CD on insomnia, twice per day, morning and night, and within a week I was sleeping like a baby. Well, better than a baby, because I'd not wake up every few hours screaming for milk!

Insomnia, Bruxism, Restless Legs Syndrome, bed wetting, sleep walking – these are just some of the sleep problems that millions of people around the country face day in and day out. Even worse, many of the victims aren't aware that they're suffering from one until the effects like fatigue and restlessness become really pronounced.

(Well, people do notice bedwetting, and I do have a MP3 for that, it's not funny and it happens)

By now you know the good news: hypnosis, also known as hypnotherapy, is often hailed as one of the best natural treatments for these disorders.   Powerful!

Even if drugs work, they are expensive, and have side-effects.

Now, to be honest, big-pharma has not studied hypnosis or measured it when it comes to treating insomnia as well as other sleep-related problems.

If they did, and were forced to publish their findings, their stock price would fall faster than a toupee in a hurricane.

I can tell you that there is existing research hinting that hypnosis could be of great use when it comes to sleeping better and getting more out of your bed time, yet you won't read it on the front page of your newspaper.

So How Does Hypnosis Affect Sleep?

We already know that just being in a hypnotic state of mind provides experiences of deep relaxation, greater suggestibility, and focused attention, so implanting a successful desire for sleep is quite simple.

Thanks to its ability to increase responsiveness, hypnosis has been frequently used to alter behaviors, emotions, as well as just plain sleeping.

Hypnotherapy, whether done at home or with a hypnotherapist, can help a patient suffering from chronic sleep problems by redirecting the patient's attention away from anxiety…away from negative thoughts that make sleeping hard as climbing a mountain with bare hands and feet. BY redirecting it to positive thoughts that result in relaxation, the patients find it a whole lot easier to sleep.

If you can't sleep because of a mountain of debt, hypnosis can help you sleep. You'll wake up refreshed, and better to re-assess your situation, and most likely find a solution.

You won't find a solution if you are dog tired day in and day out.

A Closer Look at The Benefits: Ending nightmares

Along with sleep hygiene instructions, hypnotherapy can help relieve insomnia according to a research/review published in 2007. Along with that, this review also discovered that hypnosis can be very useful in getting rid of nightmares, sleep walking and sleep terrors, bedwetting, and more.

Plus, in another report published in the same year, scientists took note of the promise hypnosis shows in treating sleep disorders. They even stated that 'there is an immediate need for researching and evaluating the efficacy of hypnotherapy in managing sleep disturbance'.

What Does It Mean To You?

If you are someone who is suffering from chronic sleep problems – insomnia, bed wetting, sleep walking, and a host of other conditions, this is definitely good news!

BUT here's a word of warning: make sure that your sleep troubles are not symptoms of a deeper medical condition like sleep apnea, which is characterized by abnormal pauses in breathing and instances of unusually low breathing.

Sometimes a lack of sleep can be a hint from the body for attention, and you do need to listen to your body.

Be sure not sleeping is not a symptom of a worse problem that you are overlooking by only treating the symptom.

Always consult with your physician before tackling your sleep problems if you feel that it's not anxiety that is keeping you awake.

Your doctor may even refer you to a tried, tested, and certified hypno-therapist. And if you are the "Do It Yourself" type of person, your doctor may even recommend resources like audio CDs, books, etc. that will teach you self-hypnosis that will let you relax your way to better sleep!

Of course, you can use mine and save a fortune, but no matter whose you chose, try it, it's safe, no side-effects, and very inexpensive.

If you'd like a free Law of Attraction Hypnosis sample, just visit www.professionalastrologycenter.info – note it's .info, NOT dot 'com.'

Natural too!

Hypnosis For Cancer – Are You Serious!?

I'm as serious as a heart attack.

In late 2003 I finally hit the last straw with this lump on my neck. It slowed down my shaving.

Each time I would see a Doctor, they would say the same thing, 'well, if it's still there in 3 months come back.'

And each time I came back, a different doctor would say the same thing.

Not being a big believer in the medical profession, I did not have a regular doctor, so I'd end up seeing someone new each time. I figured if they did not think the lump on my neck serious, neither would I.

I know, you're thinking how stupid I was.

Okay, me too.

So finally one doctor told me to get ultra-sound on the lump, and that test came back 'unknown' so I was given a referral to an Ear, Nose and Throat doctor, (that was the kind of Doctor Graham Chapman, aka 'Brian' of Life of Brian, and Monty Python member was).

So I went to see this doctor, I still remember that day in November. I was dressed in a suit, looking like a million dollars because I was seeing a business client that day, who would end up paying me hundreds of thousands of dollars for helping his sales team increase their sales by over 15 to 18%.

Anyway, when the Doctors people saw me, they rushed me to the head of the line, and asked me why I was there.

When I handed the doctor my referral, he laughed and said they all thought I was a pharmaceutical sales person, and sent me to the back of the line.

I laughed too, but it made me realize just how powerful big-pharma is.

It was long after 5 when I got to see the doctor, and within a few minutes, he told me I think you have cancer, 'right here, under your tongue.'

I looked in disbelief.

He said 'I can yank some out and test it for you, it will take 2 hours, you can go home and wait for my office, or I'll send it to the lab now and we can deal with it right away.'

I opted to wait, and figured that it would end up being a big nothing.

After all, I was very healthy, I ate right, went to the gym, didn't smoke and was a nutrition nut, (in a good way).

After two hours, I got word to see him, and was told it was the big C.

He picked up the phone, called another hospital, and got in direct to an Oncologist whom he knew.

"Brian, I have another one, you better see this guy first thing, it looks very advanced."

Long story short, it was stage 4, throughout my neck and lower part of my face, and I was told they would do chemo, radiation, and a lot of it, and it may work or it may not.

No time for 2nd opinions, (I could now see the daily exponential growth of the cancer almost doubling in size right in my mirror, so I went for it).

No guarantees: I was told to get 'your affairs in order'.

Well, rather than that, I created my own set of cancer self-hypnosis programs, which I believe was the slight edge that is the reason I'm alive today.

I can't prove it, not do I expect you to accept my belief one way or another. Except I'm here.

You see, whatever form of treatment you use, from natural to chemical to radiation, I believe hypnosis can help each of these treatments work better, faster and with more results.

And why not?   The cost of these treatments are in the thousands, whereas one CD album is only $20 or so.

Why not get a slight edge in your cancer treatment?

Why does it work?   Well, let's cover that.

Remember, hypnosis, an altered state of consciousness identified with deep relaxation, focused attention, and high suggestibility, has been proven to be a safe medical procedure by the American Medical Association since back in 1958.

And, thanks to its ability to heighten responsiveness, hypnosis is often used successfully to positively change behaviors and get rid of habits and thoughts that usually results in health issues.

"But hypnosis helping cancer patients, are you serious!?"

If that's what you are thinking read on McDuff.

Let's take a deeper look at hypnosis and what the studies about its effects to cancer patients have to say.

How Does It Work As a Part of a Treatment?

Hypnotherapy is the use of hypnosis in the treatment of different health conditions like addiction to nicotine, unhealthy weight gain, stress, social anxiety, and those are just to name a few.

Contrary to popular belief, hypnotherapists are NOT the ones in control during a hypnotherapy session.

Matter of fact, one of the main goals of hypnotherapy is to help you, the subject or patient, gain GREATER control over your behavior, your emotions, as well as bodily functions.

Pretty sure you'd agree that no matter what condition you are being treated for – maybe it is as serious as cancer or recovering from stress and anxiety, giving you greater control of your behaviors and steering it towards a positive goal is something that will greatly benefit you!

What Studies Revealed

Now, the scientific evidence to support the claim that hypnosis can help fight cancer is very minimal. However, hypnotherapy has been revealed to offer a host of benefits to cancer patients as well as survivors. Let's see what the studies have to say about it:

Cancer Surgery and Hypnotherapy

Back in 2007, a study involving 200 women who underwent breast cancer surgery showed that using hypnosis before surgery significantly reduced the amount of anesthesia needed during the operation.

Along with that, the level of pain reported afterwards along with the time and overall cost of the procedure also dropped by a sizeable amount. Matter of fact, compared to those who consulted a psychologist before their surgery, women who underwent 15 minutes of hypnosis experienced less nausea, fatigue as well as emotional upset after the procedure.

Reducing the Setbacks of Chemotherapy

Another research published in 2007 shows that hypnotherapy could significantly reduce the negative effects of chemotherapy, which includes nausea and vomiting. This research involved 6 randomized and controlled trials, and five of these trials involved pediatric cancer patients.

I can tell you, that chemo really is the ^%$#* to deal with, (and so is radiation).

Helping Breast Cancer Survivors with Hypnotherapy

Hot flashes – these are one of the pains that a breast cancer survivor needs to put up with. But here's some good news: According to a study in 2008 involving 60 women with a primary history of breast cancer, hypnotherapy can significantly reduce the number and intensity of these hot flashes.

The 5-week study showed that patients who underwent hypnosis – involving 50-minute sessions with a hypnotherapist as well as instructions for self-hypnosis at home, experienced a 68% reduction in the frequency and severity of hot flashes. On average, these patients who underwent hypnotherapy had an average of 4.39 fewer hot flashes everyday…not to mention they also showed significant improvements in anxiety, depression, and sleep.

These are just some of what big-pharma is willing to tell us.

But if other studies on the power of the brain during trance states are anything to go by, the power of hypnotic suggestion that your treatment will be 100% effective makes all the difference in my book.

Studies have shown that if the brain really believes that a treatment can work, even placebos can cure.

For me, it's all about having that low cost, natural, slight edge – a slight edge that can make a treatment much, much more effective.

It's been well over 10 years since my stage 4 cancer, and I remain cancer free.

If you'd like a free Law of Attraction Hypnosis sample, just visit www.professionalastrologycenter.info – note it's .info, NOT dot 'com.'

Hypnotherapy and Smoking Cessation –
How Hypnosis Can Help You Quit the Habit

News Flash: Smoking and hospitalized patients are more likely to quit with the help of hypnosis than using other stop-smoking methods.

How likely?

Let's see. One new study revealed that smoking patients that participated in a multi-component hypnotherapy session enjoy higher chances of a successful quit for 6 months than someone who is using Nicotine Replacement Therapy (NRT for short) or smokers who quit 'cold turkey' (which has a very low success rate...below 5 percent).

There's no doubt about it. Numerous research and studies revealed that hypnotherapy, done the right way, is a very effective way of dropping the habit.

But have you noticed the keyword above? "Done the right way" – smoking cessation hypnotherapy needs to be done correctly for it to deliver the desired effect. So what is this effective form of hypnotherapy that can help you stop nicotine addiction for good? Read on!

Different Forms of Hypnosis – Which Is the Real Deal?

There is classical hypnosis (direct suggestions), NLP (Neuro Linguistic Programming), and other forms of hypnosis. Which of these hypnotic forms are effective in stopping smoking, and which ones should you drop from your list of options?

As it turns out, other forms of hypnosis are not adequate. Such is the direct form of hypnosis. Scripted suggestions or classical hypnosis doesn't deliver that much in terms of long-term smoking cessation.

But don't fret! Other forms of hypnosis, ones that integrate elements of cognitive and behavioral therapy, have been found to be very effective.

To Be Forewarned is to be Forearmed!

Here's the thing: many hypnotherapists employ the simple/direct suggestion script for stopping smoking. To make matters worse, there are some
reports of subjects where they were treated by hypnotherapists that read
a script on a paper right in front of them...and even leave the room as
they play a recorded script. Clearly, this is not a very professional thing
to do.

On the contrary, many modern researchers and professional hypnotherapists, evidence-based practitioners, agree that direct verbal suggestion
is the bedrock of hypnotherapy.

Multi-Component Hypnotherapy – Hypnosis Combined With Behavior-
al/Cognitive Therapy

Since there is no single (or uni-modal) hypnotherapy that can be really
effective for smoking cessation, the general consensus among psychologists, experts in smoking cessation, and hypnotherapists is that a
package or a combination of different techniques specifically geared
towards quitting smoking is the most effective way to go.

Cognitive-behavioral therapy for smoking cessation, combined with
hypnosis, (also known as multi-component hypnotherapy) usually
involves a wide range of interventions that have been cut and dried to
tackle the problem – nicotine addiction and different associations made
with smoking. Such an approach attacks the problem at different levels.

Cognitive and Behavioral Hypnotherapy (CBH) is a complex but very
effective treatment. Cognitive/Behavioral Therapy, on its own, has been
tried and tested in boosting the positive effects of any stop smoking
program...may it be the use of NRTs, quitting cold turkey, etc. The
inclusion of hypnosis has been observed to improve outcomes as well.

And what do you get? A very effective combination of tailored CBT and
hypnosis therapy that gets the job done like no other form of hypnosis
can.

If you have always wanted to quit smoking but don't want to depend on
E-cigs, NRTs, and other tools for relief...and want to spare yourself the
pain of nicotine withdrawals, this is the answer.

Bottom line is this: in order to quit smoking, or other deeply chemical based addictive habit, you need to really focus on the task. Like Cancer, my opinion, based on working with people who wanted to quit, was to have them listen to a stop smoking MP3, twice per day, to put them into the correct mindset for quitting, and at the same time, have them smoke one less cigarette per day, or if that was too much, one less per every four days, eventually they were down so far that quitting was easy.

But when this was done without listening to the CD or MP3, the client did returned back to smoking as soon as they were far enough down to impact their addiction.

You must work on the mind AND the chemical need to really quit.

If you'd like a free Law of Attraction Hypnosis sample, just visit www.professionalastrologycenter.info – note it's .info, NOT dot 'com.'

You are foolish to NOT use every advantage you can to achieve your own goals.

Hypnotherapy and Weight Loss - 5 BIG Reasons Why Hypnosis Can Help Anyone Drop Those Unwanted Pounds

This is one of the biggest challenges for most folks I deal with.

Excess pounds.

Being around long before carb and calorie counting (beating them by a few centuries), hypnosis is a tool that has been around for longer than you can remember. However, very few have taken note of this age-old, attention-sharpening-and-focusing technique as an integral part of a weight loss strategy.

Back then, the scientific evidence to support the legitimate claims of even the most respected hypnotherapists has been very minimal. Plus, the stage hypnotists, the not-so-medically-helpful of hypnotherapists, didn't boost hypnosis' reputation.

Heck! Even in the mid-nineties where 18 hypnotic studies were reanalyzed...studied where clients learned the ropes of self-hypnosis and lost two times more than those who didn't...hypnotherapy remained as a secret for dropping off those unwanted and unwelcomed pounds.

BUT here's the thing: you already know the secret! And if you are not convinced of this weight loss 'secret', the 5 BIG reasons why hypnosis is effective for losing weight will get your head nodding.

You need an edge!

The world promotes eating like never before. 'All you can eat,' 'buy one get another bucket half price,' and happy appetizer hours in bars.

There is no doubt that losing weight is not easy, especially since we are genetically programed to want more calories and to NOT lose them.

So I get it. It's hard, so you DO need an edge, (or your clients do).

The Solution Is Within You

Not another crash diet...not another appetite suppressant – everything you need to succeed in your weight loss endeavors is within you! Slimming down isn't really about the latest or the fastest...it's about trusting your own, innate abilities. It's just like riding a bicycle.

Perhaps you don't know how afraid you were when you first tried to ride your bike. However, you kept practicing until you nailed it down...riding it automatically without any hiccups. Perhaps, losing weight right now seems way beyond you...yet after finding your balance through hypnosis, you will surely find your balance.

Focus On the Positive

Negative suggestions and mental approaches such as: "Doughnuts will just make you sick" will work...for a while! However, when it comes to losing weight, you want to keep those pounds off. You want something that works in the long run. And to get that, you need positive reinforcement.

Let's face it, you will not believe things that are not true, and donuts will not make us sick, unless that's all we eat.

One of the most effective and positive hypnotic suggestions has been devised by a hypnotherapist tandem of father and son, Dr. Herbert and Dr. David Spiegel:

"For my body, too much food is damaging. I need my body to live. I owe my body respect and protection."

You can use this positive and upbeat mantra...or you can use something that's your own...something that you can understand and, more importantly, relate to on a personal level.

That's the kind of positive upbeat message I use on all of my weight loss MP3s.

What's Imaginable Is Possible

If you can imagine it, it will come! This is one of the cornerstones of hypnosis. Athletes gearing up for a competition prepare themselves by visualizing victory. In the same vein, visualizing healthy eating gears you up for a fitter and healthier life ahead.

If you find it too tough to imagine, no problem; just dig up an old photograph when you are still happy and comfortable with your figure. Remember all of the things you did back then. Resurrect those healthy routines you did day in and day out.

Have 2 Strategies!

Two heads are better than one. Surely, you are familiar with that old adage. In the same manner, two strategies are better than one! When it comes to shedding off those pounds and keeping your slim and healthy figure, having a combination of cognitive-behavioral therapy (CBT) as well as hypnotherapy is the most effective way.

Clients who undergo both, according to research, lose twice as much weight and don't fall back to their old and weight-gaining habits.

In Conclusion...

Hypnosis is more than just about stage performance – making other people walk on burning coal or cluck like chickens. Drop those excess pounds with hypnotherapy and keep them off NOW!

Or, just go on a good solid diet program while listening – twice a day – to a good weight loss MP3. Your mind undergoing the change won't let you down. But don't stop listening for at least a year after you have lost what weight you want.

It's all inside you – that you must change.

If you'd like a free Law of Attraction Hypnosis sample, just visit www.professionalastrologycenter.info – note it's .info, NOT dot 'com.'

Relieve Stress And Anxiety With Self-Hypnosis NOW!

Hypnosis has helped A LOT of people reduce stress and anxiety... allowing them to zone in on their goals and perform better at the physical and mental tasks they face day in and day out.

So why aren't you using it!? True, many people are using hypnotherapists to guide them, but do you know that you can also do it yourself from the comfort of your own home?

In your office?

On a commuter train to or from work?

On a bus taking your team to the next game, or taking your band to your next gig.

It's about time you take advantage of this very powerful stress management tool today, and you can do so by following the next easy steps, which should only take 5 to 30 minutes of your time.

Here's how:

- Look for a quiet place, one that is free from distractions and will allow you to focus on the session ahead.

- Get into a comfy position, but not one that makes you fall asleep. Others like to recline, some prefer to sit on a cozy chair, while there are some who are really comfortable lying down. Don't be afraid to experiment and see what works best for you.

- Decide what you want to achieve for this session, and make sure you put it into a positive statement. You see, the subconscious mind doesn't register negatives.

For example, if you want to get rid of stress and anxiety, instead of saying "I'm feeling less and less stressful by the minute" go for "I'm getting more and more relaxed as time goes by".

For the first statement, the mind won't reinforce the word "less" and would focus on the word "stressful", which is something you want to get rid of! The second statement, on the other hand, is positive…allowing your mind to focus on the word "relax".

- Next, start breathing deeply and slowly – expanding your tummy when you inhale instead of raising your shoulders. For extra positive effect, imagine that you are breathing in calmness and relaxation, and exhaling out the stress you have experienced throughout the day.

- Moving forward, pick and imagine an environment that you find relaxing. It's different for everyone – it can be a beach, a natural cave, their bedroom, etc. Imagine going further and deeper into it.

Visualize yourself walking a long road leaving your current stressful surroundings behind with the restless noise slowly fading away in the background.

At first, you may not feel anything different…you may not get that "WOW" moment. But keep on practicing it and you should get there in no time. It's very much like the state you feel when you are day-dreaming or in deep concentration.

- When you are done and feeling really relaxed…far away from the regular and usually stressful life we all live, start repeating the positive phrase/goal you opted for in the initial steps. You may want to see the words come to life, focus on how they sound, or better yet, vividly visualize – complete with sights and sounds, the desired outcome.

When you are completely relaxed and feeling far from your regular life, begin repeating the positive phrase you chose for this session. You may choose to visualize the words, focus on their sound in your head, or visualize the end result.

Relieving yourself of the stress and anxiety you experienced throughout the day doesn't have to be complicated. All you need is some free time along with a quiet place, clothes you are comfy with, an open mind, and a very clear idea of what you want to achieve and you are good to go!

Now, if you are willing to do this first thing when you awake, and as the last thing before you fall asleep, you are going to get much more from it, as you are already in a near perfect state.

If you don't want to worry about creating your own set of desires, just use someone else's, in the form of a MP3 or CD. Professionals like me create these, they are a bargain, and give you an unfair advantage that others will never have.

Really, today, with the power of a smart phone, you can have a library – let me correct that – you MUST have a library of hypnosis MP3s to re-mold you into the best you can be at... you decide!

From cooking to sex, from getting your degree, to learning French, all can be yours!

Yours for pennies!

If you'd like a free Law of Attraction Hypnosis sample, just visit www.professionalastrologycenter.info – note it's .info, NOT dot 'com.'

Hypnotherapy for Social Anxiety – Getting Rid Of Those Jitters and Overcoming Shyness

It was back in 1700s when the first research about hypnosis (originally termed as animal magnetism) was set in motion by Franz Anton Mesmer. However, it wasn't until 1958 when the American Medical Association (or AMA) acknowledged hypnotherapy's validity as a very useful medical procedure.

Fast forward today, hypnotherapy, usually combined with Cognitive/Behavioral Therapy (or CBT), has been one of the tried and tested 'tools' for stopping smoking, alleviating pain and physical conditions like asthma and IBS, and those are just to name a few.

And just recently, another discovery has been made concerning new uses of hypnotherapy...that of relieving social anxiety and shyness. If you are someone who tends to cower for no apparent reason when talking to strangers or stutter a lot when speaking in public, this may be just the 'pill' you need.

Getting Rid Of Social Anxiety through Hypnotherapy – How It Works

"The events and experiences we undergo are linked to physical and emotional reactions."

This is the premise of hypnotherapy. When we experience the same events once again, the physical reactions and emotions we have subconsciously linked to it (regardless if it's healthy or not) are brought back to the surface...reactivated.

Here's a simple example: Let's say someone just had a traumatic public speaking experience. Perhaps, in the middle of his speech, he forgot his piece. He felt lost...he panicked in front of hundreds or even thousands of people. Such a person is very likely to experience the negative/unhealthy emotions when speaking again in public or shaking hands with other people. His subconscious has linked public speaking to panic and confusion.

Using the simple example above, the goal of hypnotherapy is to break that link…to separate the traumatic public speaking experience from the negative emotions he came to associate with it. Furthermore, during these hypnotherapy sessions, the therapist might even give post hypnotic suggestions that will allow the subject to relax whenever he wants.

What Happens In a Hypnotherapy Session

Before a therapist starts a hypnotherapy session, he will first discuss your medical history – looking at and discussing the problems with you, while providing you with a simple overview of how the process works.

Just in case you are worried like I was, no, the goal of hypnotherapy isn't to make you run around the room like a chicken or do weird stuff. That's stage hypnosis. What hypnotherapy tries to do is to have you enter an altered state of consciousness.

Known as trance or hypnotic state, people in this different level of consciousness experience extreme relaxation, lowered blood pressure and heart rate, as well as significant changes in brainwaves.

BUT more importantly, while in trance or hypnotic state, you will be highly responsive to suggestions. These suggestions can be direct or multi-layered. In most hypnotherapy sessions that deal with social anxiety, the latter has been found to work a lot better than the former.

These suggestions – its delivery and structure, will serve as the main tool of the hypnotherapist in breaking down the negative associations and anchors to social events and interactions you have unknowingly made.

At the end of every session, the hypnotherapist will bring you back to alertness and will discuss and reflect on the experience with you.

No pills, no pain – if that sounds like a great way to finally get rid of social anxiety, maybe it's about time you give hypnotherapy the shot it deserves.

Bottom Line: no matter what is holding you back from seizing the day, the week, the year, your life, you will not move forward until you eliminate or conquer it.

Hypnosis works.

Just find someone skilled to deal with it for you, or find a CD that has been made for problems such as yours.

Don't fall into the trap that you are 'different' – trust me, most people have the same fears that you have, and there is a program out there made for you.

From shyness to sales, from golf to stuttering, from losing weight, to body image, from working out to becoming hard working.

I have grown so much thru creating my own sets, and helping hundreds, thousands of others with my CDs.

If you don't want mine, find a set you like better.

Most people in this field are professional.

If I can be of help in any way, please just reach out to me.

Best, David Anton

If you'd like a free Law of Attraction Hypnosis sample, just visit www.professionalastrologycenter.info – note it's .info, NOT dot 'com.'

This is a little part of what I offer my clients via my trusted partners, iTunes, Apple Music, Spotify, Google Play, AmazonMP3, Rhapsody, eMusic and MediaNet

How would you like a Guaranteed Method to become a success in your field?

And no, this is NOT another course, training, boot-camp or expensive coaching.

What if you suddenly loved doing the boring, but important part of your tasks and had an attitude that was invincible and your leadership and confidence was overflowing to others?

It can be yours.

How would you like to suddenly turn your business or life around, so you become successful no matter what you are doing? From going to school, learning to be a great athlete, a great law student, success in business, romance, or getting over an illness?

If you know what you want, and are sure of it, well relax, there is an answer.

There is a simple solution that will unleash your ability to have the same confidence, power, leadership and success or strength that anyone who has mastered what you want too.

Sound crazy, it's not – its science.

What this is NOT:

Not more training

Not 'coaching'

Not an ebook

Not a membership site full of endless videos

Not a guru

And even NOT expensive!

First, before you read any further, be honest with yourself, because if you answer YES to the following question, we can help you:

If you think you can achieve your goal on your own, why haven't you by now?

If your honest opinion is 'I can't' then we CAN help you, and we guarantee it.

There is a reason why THEY succeed at getting what they want. It's not luck, chance, insider info, intelligence or even somebody's 'system', it's that 99% of the time these Winners have an unbeatable attitude for success or leadership or health.

NOW before you think this is some sort of 'training' program for your attitude – let me tell you it's 100% not.

Look, let's be frank. If you have the suspicion that you don't have that same confidence to get past your problem, you do need a mental edge.

But you don't need another training! You don't need to go to a coach, or mentor, or just go to one more expensive 'special course'.

What if we could change your attitude and confidence level, your ability for your body to 'self-heal' or give you the ability to achieve any think you want?

What if there was a way for you to quickly get that 'Zen like' mental edge that will have you diverting wasted mental energy into becoming a laser beam focused tool to create the brain you need to get what you want?

And what if you could do it right away, quickly, and for such a low cost that you could not pass up this guaranteed offer?

Take 2 minutes to change your life and read this important information.

To be a successful means being in the 'Success Zone' – traits like:

•   LOVING to focus – just plain old LOVING to get to your work or studying, or practicing!

•   Not caring about what others say and moving on quickly

•   Quickly detecting if an action you take will be positive or negative

•   Success in relationships, finding the right person, both for business, learning, healing and love

•   Being in Mental Top shape to deal with all of your problems

•   Having your brain Tuned up for Practical Answers

•   Total brain optimization for recognition of positive paths that you should follow

Would you like to find a way to move directly into 'Success Zone' too?

The 'Zone', that Winning Mindset, that special person's Edge, where your subconscious takes over and acts faster than you can act, seizes control over your day, has all the answers, the confidence, knows how to deal with negative people – in short being the person you NEED to become. It's all inside you if you want to unleash it.

Want proof?

Have you ever met or listened to trainers explain their stuff? Most of the time, you come away feeling like, 'that's not really anything I've not thought for myself or heard before'. In fact, after you 'learned' the basics for self-mastery - the only REAL difference between you and a successful networker is the time or experience that they have.

But what happens over time?

Like any thing you do, eventually you can learn it so well, that it is now instinctual, you can do it without consciously thinking. That is the key. All successful people had their brain adjusted BY many years of trial and error. But once their mindset was perfect, their success caught fire!

Remember the last time you drove home from the office and you got out of your car, and could not even remember details of the drive home? That is because your subconscious mind was able to perform most of the actions for you. Perhaps you were deep in thought, or talking on the phone, but you were trusting your subconscious mind to take you safely home, and it did.

Simple, yet POWERFUL – some people can't drive a car with ALL their attention – yet you could and not even remember the trip home! That means you can let your subconscious take over once you've pro-grammed it.

This is the Zen edge that the Master Achievers have, sometimes they don't even know it, sometimes they think it's some secret system or talent that only they have, but it's not. It's just that they now perform in the Success Zone, that mental state of consciousness where the sub-conscious has taken charge.

For a Master Achiever performing in the Zone, their subconscious mind sees the subtle but clear signals that tells them what to do, creates a love for it if it's a dull task, and these Master Achievers working in the Zone quickly know if they are wasting time or are doing what they need to.

Their subconscious quickly recalls similar situations – patterns, and provides them with the answers to questions, remembers what to do without feeling anything but good about the whole process. They sound and are confident.

You can achieve this same confident mindset – you can move into the 'Master Achiever Success Zone' too and you can do it quickly, without all the time it takes for trainings, practice, and mentorship – and we guaran-tee it. You see, you have heard all the phrases before, you have taken the trainings, read the books, downloaded ebooks, listened to mentors, by now your subconscious has the answers, it's all in you already – all that needs to be done is to unleash it from within you so it works in real-time, and that's our guarantee.

How many times have you said to yourself, 'oh, I should have said this or that'? You KNOW the answers, you know the training, you just need your brain's powerful subconscious to take over and provide you with the answers in REAL time when you need it, not after you lost your health, the person of your dreams or whatever your goal is.

How can you speed up the process and get into the Success Zone now?

How can you make use of your lighting fast subconscious mind and use its powerful pattern recognizing 'software' that will stop your procrastination and get you moving toward your goal?

How do you tap into what you already know?

What would it be worth to you to suddenly turn your LIFE around, so you become as successful as your secret idol?

Introducing the amazing state-of-the-art Master Achiever Mind Training Hypnosis system.

That's where the Master Achievers Mind Training program takes over for you.

It will eliminate from your mind all the negative experiences of the past, the years of hearing 'NO', or your perception that 'no one wants' to help you now, or that you can't win, can't meet a target, reach a goal, find health, or your soul mate. This program will prevent these feelings from getting in your way, and in turn, it will change your attitude into those who in the Success Zone have:

•   LOVE to connect with new people,

•   Enhance and magnify all your knowledge and training so you can call on that knowledge in real time, not after you needed it,

•   See patterns from the past so you can anticipate so you know what to do in each set of circumstances,

•   Display total confidence and exude power and leadership so much that no one will ask you about your past – your voice and inflections will present such success that people will assume you are a top performer and want to give you their business and referrals, or love and friendship

•   Be at peace with your life, not afraid of it, but instead look forward to each day

That's the power of self-hypnosis.

Just sit back and listen; on your computer, your iPod, iPad or other MP3 player, or even on a CD player if you like. The more you listen, the more powerful and effective you will become.

How does it work?

Through a scientific technique called Brain Entrainment and Specific Affirmation based Self-Hypnosis.

While you sit back and listen to your Master Achiever Training Hypnosis tracks, this powerful program uses specific, positive commands sent DIRECTLY to both your conscious and subconscious mind, commanding it into becoming a powerful pattern recognizing 'Mindware', to take-over whatever challenge you have, and reach whatever goal you seek

What others say:

David Williams MLM Author, author of The Only Mindset Book You'll Ever Need for Network Marketing Success has this to say:

Without doubt, the mind is our most important asset for networking success – I searched for years for a variable to make a difference until I found this set of Hypnosis Audios. They work. Don't ignore these because they're not expensive, their profoundly valuable. They make a great gift to your team leaders too. I can tell you, I've sent many copies to my leaders. Plug them in, and change your prospecting life!

Order today.

What is it like?

First you will hear a hypnotic message to get you into the right state of mind, relaxed and ready to accept the family, health, business and life changing messages to come.

Once you are in a receptive, relaxed state, your 'gatekeeper' is not on guard, and as such, now your program starts to deliver directly specific messages to your conscious and subconscious mind.

Hypnotic mindseeding works better, faster and more effectively than using 'Will Power', or the conscious mind, or even reading positive affirmations aloud to yourself. And this program is cheaper than attending 'the next BIG training!'

This is the most affordable way to achieve peace, health, success, love, friendship or repair relationships.

Let's See What Other People Are Saying...

Sadly, I was a heavy smoker - so I started using the Stop Smoking Mindware Program for just 31 days - **and QUIT cold turkey**! That was 10 months ago - so when I saw these MLM programs I was first in, I had proof they worked! I can tell you, this Sales & Prospecting Subliminal is the best investment ever - belongs on every networker's iPod!

Rate:

Feedback From Real People!

John Macy, Oakland, MD
www.total-game-changer.com/1482347

Take a look at some more titles below.

David Anton

Each of these titles can be found on iTunes, Amazon, or most other music providers.

Search by Title, or, Search 'Rapid Hypnosis Success'

Men Only: Exclusive Hypnosis Portfolio for Men ONLY!

Women Only: Exclusive Hypnosis Portfolio for Today's Woman

Business:

Corporate & Career, Personal Success Exclusive Hypnosis Portfolio

Success in Business Hypnosis Personal Makeover Transformation Collection

Learning:

Learning - Language, School, Exams Exclusive Hypnosis Portfolio

Success and Wealth:

Success Personality Transformational Hypnosis Collection

Wealth: Money, Income and Financial Success Hypnosis Collection

Law of Attraction & Abundance Hypnosis Collection

Power Personality Makeover Hypnosis Collection

Relationships:

Sex, Love, You & Relationships - Exclusive Hypnosis Portfolio

Health:

Health: Heart, Cancer, Diabetes, Arthritis and More Exclusive Hypnosis Portfolio

END: Phobias Allergies Addictions Pain Anxiety and Unhealthy Worry Exclusive Hypnosis Portfolio

Anti-Aging:

Longevity, Revitalize and Rejuvenate - Exclusive Hypnosis Portfolio

Esoteric:

Mystical Psychic - Extrasensory Results Exclusive Hypnosis Portfolio

Spiritual Karmic: Universal Energy Exclusive Hypnosis Portfolio

Sport:

Body Excellence - Sport, Fitness, Exercise Exclusive Hypnosis Portfolio

Sales:

Car - Auto Sales & Prospecting Pack

Real Estate Sales & Prospecting Pack

Insurance Sales & Prospecting Pack

Day Trading:

Get Into The Trading Zone! - FOREX and Online Trading

Network Marketing:

Network Marketing Rapid Mindset Hypnosis Success - Volume 1

Network Marketing Rapid Mindset Hypnosis Success - Volume 2

Network Marketing Rapid Mindset Hypnosis Success - Volume 3

Network Marketing Rapid Mindset Hypnosis Success - Volume 4

Network Marketing Rapid Mindset Hypnosis Success - Volume 5

Internet Marketing:

Internet Marketing Rapid Success Hypnosis System - Volume 1

Internet Marketing Rapid Success Hypnosis System - Volume 2

Order safely through our partners:

iTunes, Apple Music, Spotify, Google Play, AmazonMP3, Rhapsody, eMusic and MediaNet

Are you struggling to get clients and build your Esoteric practice?

Do you find that potential clients just disappear?

Are you ready to REALLY take your practice seriously and help people with your arts?

If so, you Need this Book if you are an Astrologer, if you are a Clairvoyant, if you are a Shaman, if you are a Tarot reader, if you are a Medium, if you are a Diviner, if you are a Psychic, if you are a Mystic, if you are a Spiritualist, if you are a Seer or any kind of Esoteric Specialist.

If you're any kind of an Esoteric worker and want to find a way to get more clients, practice your gift with more people, have those in need find you and desire to listen to you, and welcome you to be their practitioner and stop 'guru seeking' then you need to follow the simple steps outlined in this book.

Would you like your potential clients pre-sold on you?

No matter what you know, practice and deliver, if your potential client thinks you are 'just like anyone else' you will not achieve your potential of helping others.

Welcome to all the shortcuts, insider branding methods, and Internet secrets for pre-qualifying prospects that all the big guru's use, and you can too.

What is the difference between you and successful practitioner?

Why is it that they can take on new client after new client and you can't?

The science of what we practice is the same, but there is one thing missing: How your client perceives you.

Why?

Because, whether they know it or not, successful practitioner come across as experts.

Either consciously or unconsciously, they come across with authority and communicate from a position of strength. This is what you are going to learn and do.

When you are the expert, your entire posture over the phone will change, in person will change, when offering to do a reading will change, over Skype will change.

Why?

Because when you know that your prospective client is pre-disposed to believe and respect you - your delivery changes.

Your prospect feels good about you, and feels privileged to follow you. They WANT to be guided by you. By being an 'expert' or authority, you will find building your practice a charm, not a chore.

When you follow the simple steps is outlined in this book, you will find clients happy to hear from you.

Coming to you for answers, not taking a step without you!

Why?

Because in their eyes, you are a 'someone.'

Think of it this way: right now, prior to setting yourself up as an expert or an authority, you are floating in the ocean as one of a million other drops of water, each one saying the same thing, offering your guidance to everyone. If they ask you, 'why should I listen to you?' you'll say 'It's not about me, it's about you, and the charts or....' OR.... ...you are someone who has wisely invested in this book.

You have decided to take matters into your own hands, and create a situation where your prospect is already sold on consulting with you.

You will sound strong on the phone, and speak from a position of author-ity and strength, because you know you appear strong.

Your prospective clients are impressed, will take your calls, follow up with you, and, you'll find rejection disappears and struggling ends.

As an expert, there is no more 'hard selling', as you become irresistibly attractive to those in need. If you are ready to become irresistibly attractive you're ready to Brand Yourself - order today and Get Started!

Order it today on Amazon and get known, get working, and get busy!

How to Brand yourself as an Astrologer so you can get more Clients and Earn what you are worth!: This simple 9 step method works for any Esoteric Practitioner

http://www.amazon.com/Brand-yourself-Astrologer-Clients-worth/dp/151734526X